Because of May 10th, 1980;
The Flamingo Incident

Because of May 10th, 1980; The Flamingo Incident

Cladwell Farrington

To order additional copies of this book, contact:
Xlibris
844-714-8691
www.Xlibris.com
Orders@Xlibris.com
828971

Contents

Dedication

This book is dedicated to my wife, Genester Farrington for her loving support, and being the manager of this project. It is also dedicated to our daughters, Claudine Cartwright and Dawn Farrington Smith, to the memory of our daughter, Nakia, and my late parents, Cladwell Sr. and Rhona Farrington, the four fallen men of the HMBS Flamingo, to my fellow survivors and the Bahamian people. Special dedication to the daughter of Austin Smith who was born after his death. Also, former Commodore Clifford Scavella, a fellow son of Hatchet Bay, Eleuthera, whose dream was bigger than mine.

Acknowledgement

I wish to also acknowledge the contributions of the following persons, who without their assistance, this book would not have become a reality. My sincerest thank you.

J. Shannell Evans and her assistant, Corrine Evans – Editors
Reporters of the Tribune and the Nassau Guardian
The Department of Archives, Nassau, Bahamas
Royal Bahamas Defence Force
Bahamas Information Services
Mr. Kishan Munroe – cover photo
Mrs. Pammy Gibson – Typist, Eleuthera

Hon. Philip Bethel, Mrs. Levada Ingraham, Mrs. Myrtis Newton, Rev. Eric Johnson, Denny Seymour, Mrs. Rose Wood, Kimble and Ron Wood, Mrs. Florence Scavella, Franky Durham and Thaddeus Paul.

I further acknowledge my brothers and my late sisters, Pastor Arlene Isaacs and Chyrle Shelly Johnson, Mrs. Loretta Jacques, Hazel Carey, Rhona Hutchinson Pinder, Edna Symonette, Mrs. Stella Randall, the Eleuthera communities, the late Mrs. Delores Ingraham who believed in me to fix anything, Mrs. Lida Scavella, Unka Bo, Wellington Kemp, Craig Kemp, Mark Thompson and family, Tyrone Murphy, Gaye Carol Davis, Leon Johnson, Carmetta Stuart, friends, and co-workers.

This book could not be a success without the hardworking typing pool; the clerical staff at the Defence Force who did the typing of my terrible handwriting: Mrs. Delores Pratt, Mrs. Florence Coleby, Mrs. Cleomi Turner, and Cinderita McKenzie.

Also, the late Pastors Lambert Farrington and Edward J. Brown, teachers, staff, and students of the P. A. Gibson school, Jodi Pinder, Jonathan Randoll, Wanda Scavella, and Mrs. Emily Petty.

There are so many other persons to whom I owe my gratitude, but I am not able to list.

Thank you to all of you!

Introduction

I was trying to avoid writing about May 10th, 1980, but the story must be told so that others can know and appreciate what we experienced that day. Not to sadden you, but to give to you, the Bahamian people, the true story from one who lived it.

Thank God I survived to tell my story – Help me, God.

Preparation

During the week leading up to May 10th, the ship that I served on was on Call in Eleuthera. We were docked at Cape Eleuthera Hotel and Marina. We were there for three days. A By-Election was scheduled to be held for the Rock Sound Constituency after the passing of the sitting Member of Parliament, Mr. Preston Albury. A few of us were native Eleutherians; from Hatchet Bay to be exact, and we desperately desired to go home for a visit. However, our ship's Commander did not permit us to do so.

We left Eleuthera for Nassau on Thursday, May 8th, 1980. Upon our arrival, we were told that we were going out to Sea. They told us that we had about two hours to get supplies and uniforms and say goodbye to our families. Some officers decided they were not going and played sick and others said they were starting vacation. The rest of the crew, myself included, prepared for the trip to sea.

The Royal Bahamas Defense Force was officially established on March 31st, 1980, just five and a half weeks before. Our ship was the HMBS Flamingo and we prepared to leave New Providence for a ten-day trip involving the routine patrol of the Bahamian waters.

Before leaving Nassau, on Thursday, we did take the opportunity to visit family members and friends. This included wives and girlfriends as we were leaving from the Base and not from our homes. We all went out to bid goodbye to our loved ones.

John Wallace, Austin Smith, Trevor Sands, and I drove together. I dropped Smith off, and Wallace and I visited a few friends. We laughed and talked until it was time to leave, then we said goodbye and see you soon.

We stopped to collect Sands and went back to Smith's house. We waited for some time, but Smith did not come out. Just as I decided to drive off, his sister shouted that he was coming. He got into the car and we left going back to the Base at Coral Harbour.

When we arrived back at the harbour, we boarded our craft, the HMBS Flamingo to prepare for sailing. This was a 103-foot patrol vessel built in England in 1978 and brought to The Bahamas. The HMBS Flamingo along with her sister ship, HMBS Marlin had been in operation for just under two years. We sailed away at 2:30 p.m. that afternoon, excited to be serving, not knowing what we were going into. If only I knew what the end would bring as we left. One thing we were sure of, and that was, we were again on water moving.

Days Before

Being on a ship was very exciting. The H.M.B.S. Flamingo was an excellent craft. It was well kept by its crew led by Commander Amos Rolle, a native of the island of Exuma. The other crew members were:

Sub. Lieutenant, Anthony Allen — Executive Officer
Acting Sub. Lieutenant, Wilfred Sands — Navigator
Petty Officer, Peterson James — Cox'wain
Leading Mechanic, Oscar Maynard Miller — Engineer
Leading Mechanic, Gregory Curry — Electrician
Leading Mechanic, Dencil Clarke — Electrician
Able Seaman, Cladwell Farrington — Radio Operator
Able Seaman, Trevor Sands — Deckhand
Able Mechanic, Eugene Thompson — Engineer
Marine Seaman, John Wallace — Deckhand
Able Seaman, Fenrick Sturrup — Yeoman
Marine Seaman, Whitfield Neely — Deckhand
Marine Seaman, Anthony Russell — Deckhand
Marine Seaman, Willard Saunders — Cook
Marine Seaman, Leo Kirby — Cook
Marine Seaman, Austin Smith — Radio Operator
Marine Seaman, David Tucker — Gunman
Marine Seaman, Edward Williams — Deckhand

These men made up one of the finest crews one could have worked along with. We had great comradery. We laughed, fussed, talked at times, and supported each other.

I can remember the Thursday night quite well. It was the night we had a big argument about who had the most and the best-looking women. It certainly was a night. I had everyone laughing for some four hours until Smith came for me to relieve him from the radio. It was entertaining. It was "A time to laugh......"

The following day, on Friday, May 9th I never saw a group of men changed so quickly. In the Sleeping Quarters, the music was turned down very low. Those not in the Quarters asleep were someplace else reading Scripture. In the radio room, Smith working the first shift was reading his Testament. I worked the late shift after him and found his New Testament where he had left it. It was opened to St. Luke's Gospel.

After lunch, the vessel stopped and we did a little fishing. We also spotted two Cuban American pleasure crafts. We boarded and searched the boats, but they had nothing on them except for some automatic weapons. As pleasure crafts, they were allowed one to two guns for their protection.

HMBS Flamingo and Her Crew

*The Ill-Fated Defence Force Vessel HMBS Flamingo, upon arrival from Brittan in 1978
Courtesy of the Department of Archives*

https://rbdf.gov.bs/the-flamingo-incident/

https://rbdf.gov.bs/the-flamingo-incident/

Ragged Island and Sighting of Cuban Fishing Vessel

It was about 9:30 a.m. on Saturday, May 10th, 1980 when we sighted land which we were later told was Ragged Island.

If you were never there before, you would never know there is life on the island. We were all glad to know that we were going to spend some time on an island as it had been such a long time since were last on dry land. Tucker was the happiest of us all, as he wanted to go ashore to get some drinking water.

We cleaned the ship then got dressed in our finest in preparation for going ashore. A boat from Ragged Island came to take us ashore because the Flamingo was too large to enter the shallow water.

However, before we were able to leave the vessel, Commander Rolle announced, "Listen up men, I don't think we should go ashore just now. I think we should go and check out this Cay up there and come back here later." The Cay he was referring to was Cay Santo Domingo. It seemed we were being rerouted there. The mandate of the crew of the HMBS Flamingo was to curtail poaching in that area of Bahamian territorial waters. The ship's radar had detected what looked like fishing vessels in the direction of the Cay. You should have seen the look on the faces of the men after they learned we were not going ashore.

We pulled anchor and headed for Cay Santo Domingo. We spent a few minutes laughing at Wallace, who was on punishment – he had to clean brass.

As we sailed towards the direction of the Cay, Tucker, Williams, Wallace, Sands, and I were looking over the side of the ship into the water. The water was so clear and calm. Suddenly a piece of land appeared ahead of us. About 500 yards north of the land, we spotted two unusual-looking boats.

"All men get to action station," was the order. Every crew member rushed off to his place of duty. We were told that the two vessels were Cuban Registered. The boats were ordered to stop over the loud hailer but they refused. They tried to escape in a southwesterly direction, so we prepared to give chase. In the haste of lowering the dory, Clarke was almost caught up under the ship and lost his gun in the process of trying not to fall.

We gave chase and showed them our flag but they continued. Warning shots were fired but they still refused. At this time, the men on the fishing vessel were shouting and making signs at us. I never saw a group of men so ill-mannered in all my life. It took us about one hour to get the boats to stop. They came to a stop when Commander Rolle gave Tucker the order to fire shots across their bow. At this time, they were almost five miles away from the Cay.

Marines comprising the boarding team were sent aboard the boats to search for signs of poaching. In Cuba, everything is Government-owned, therefore, these two fishing boats were owned by the Government. There were four males found onboard each of the two boats, and a large quantity of fish, although I couldn't say exactly what made up the catch that was found on the boat, the boats were loaded down. The men were arrested and their boats Ferrocem 165 and Ferrocem 54 were taken into tow. Their catch was also confiscated. We were not aware, however, that the men had made radio contact with Cuba.

The usual occurrence when a boat was arrested, was that the prisoners are placed aboard our boat and the captured craft towed. But in this case, the prisoners were kept onboard their boat by our officers. We spent some time trying to organize the boats for the tow back to Ragged Island. In Nassau, they would be charged and if found guilty, would have had to pay their fines or be placed in prison. A few months prior, two Cuban Registered fishing boats were intercepted and charged with poaching. I assume this was the reason for these fishing boats being reluctant to stop.

Finally, we were able to get the boats tied up for towing to make our return to Ragged Island. We were all a bit nervous because of what we had heard about the Cuban Government's reactions each time its boats were arrested.

A photo that was taken on an earlier trip. Standing is David Tucker, Leo Kirby on the right, and myself at the front. (Personal photo)

Attack of all Attacks

The Attack of All Attacks

I was still in the Radio room waiting for a reply from Base. Spinning around in the chair I looked at my watch – it was about 6:45 pm. Before I could spin again there was a loud sound and a "solid hit" that shook the vessel and the shelves of radios came tumbling down on top of me. This was followed by fire, smoke, and noise. Everything in the room where I was, was broken and my left shoulder was injured.

At that moment, only one thing came to my mind and that was to get out and get out quickly. The inside was a total wreck and I could not figure out why the men were trying to get inside instead of out.

"Hey, you'll go back out!" I shouted as I made my frantic way to the outside.

However, the scene on the outside mirrored the inside – there was fire and smoke there too. But there was also gunfire. Rapid machine gunfire fell all around. The ship's metal was melting and the vessel continued to fall apart. The loud bang had been a rocket hit. The men were just standing around not sure of where to go, what to do when to do it or even how to do it. Everyone was stunned. Shocked.

"Lord, help us all," I cried out. I saw Tucker putting on a life jacket and I wasted no time in tearing off my boots. Before anyone could say, "Jack Robinson," I was in the water and swimming at my fastest pace.

I was quite a distance ahead of everyone because I was the first person to leave the ship. At this time, the jets kept firing at the FLAMINGO putting a very large hole into it. They were Cuban military MiG fighter jets. They swooped down to us in the water firing bullets at the same time. Every time I saw them coming toward me, I dove down and stayed as long as my breath would keep me. After a while I got tired. If the jets had come my way again, I think I would have been shot, because I would have been too tired to go under again.

I came up to one of the Cuban vessels we had arrested which was some 200 yards away from the FLAMINGO and climbed aboard. Neely who had been posted on the detained craft got into the vessel's rubber dinghy and began rescuing the other men in the water. From where I was, I could see the FLAMINGO. I was sure that the crew on the bridge section with all of the navigational equipment were dead because the bridge was in flames. As I watched, I saw someone jump into the water but at that distance, I could not be sure who the person was. I later learned that the person had been Commander Rolle. He had attempted to put out the fire but it became too big for him to handle.

The jets had gone now but a Cuban military helicopter remained to hover in the area, seeming to wait for the ship to sink.

It all happened so fast – the attack, the swim, the sinking – because in what felt like minutes, the H.M.B.S. FLAMINGO, went down to the bottom of the ocean. As it was going we were still able to stand up and salute it.

https://rbdf.gov.bs/memorial-service-for-hmbs-flamingo-incident/

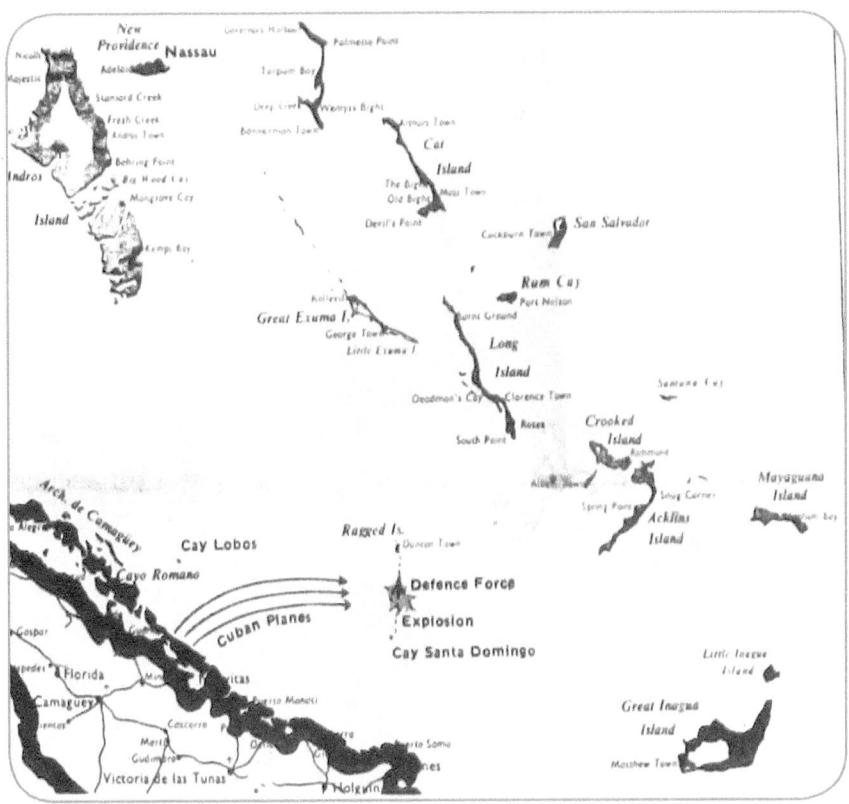

WHERE THE INCIDENT OCCURRED – This rough map shows the approximate area located some 30 miles of Ragged Island where the HMBS FLAMINGO was bombed. The map is taken from a clipping of the Tribune dated Monday, May 12th, 1980.

Courtesy of the Department of Archives

Loss of the Four
Our Four Heroes

Loss of The Four

"Where is Tucker?"

"Where are Sturrup and Smith?"

"I don't see Williams!" The cries for the missing crewmen rang out.

A search was made in the waters and the life rafts, but there was no sign of them.

Curry said that Sturrup and Smith were swimming in the back and side of him when he heard them shouting for help. He was not able to help them because he was too tired.

Thompson said that the last thing he heard Williams, who was swimming by him, say was, "Oh Lordy" – then they were not seen anymore.

A myriad of emotions washed over us. We were shaken up. We were mad. We were also very sad because four of our men were missing. Sun was now setting and that made any further search in those waters difficult. The military helicopter appeared closer with machine guns and searched around the water and life rafts for any bodies or life. After the helicopter left, we prepared to sail away from the area. Everyone was transferred to one of the Cuban vessels, the Ferrocem 165, and the other was turned loose. As night fell, we tried to sail away to seek refuge on Ragged Island but the boat was just going around in circles. We were not making any forward movement and we could see bright beams from searchlights in the distance.

Seeing the desperateness of our situation, I realized we needed God's help. If we did not get away from the area soon, our attackers would kill us all. We were at their mercy. Headquarters had not been notified of the attack to be able to send help out to us. We did not have time. The bombing had destroyed all of our essential spots on the ship; the engines, the bridge where the Captain had been, and the Radio room. It was a miracle I survived the hit. I was the only person down below at the time of the bombing and had been unaware of what was going on above deck.

I said to the others, "Guys, let's pray," and I prayed. Unknown to us, one of the Cuban captains had pulled the steering pin from the engine and threw it in the bilge; that's the oily water down in the engine room. But God answered our prayers. He guided Miller to locate the pin and put it back in place. It was only then that the fishing boat began to stop spinning and move forward and onto Ragged Island.

"Our Four Heroes"

Austin Smith

"Smithy" as he was sometimes called, was an Operator like myself on board the FLAMINGO. Before we went to sea, Smith and I left the Coral Harbour Base with a pipe and cigarette in our mouths playing around with them.

We had a good working relationship because he was very understanding. He and I rotated twelve-hour shifts. At night when his shift was ending, he would come and awaken me saying, "Farrington, your time to come on the radio now". He was liked by all of the crew members and his personality was, "one way" all the time; a saying commonly used in Bahamian colloquialism.

I will miss you a great deal – God bless your soul, Rest in Peace.

Fenrick Sturrup

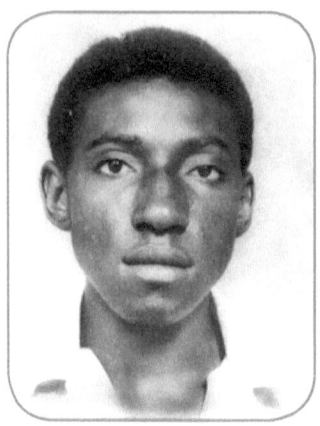

Sturrup, known to us as "Guy Smiley" was a great actor. It did not matter to him who you were or where you came from, he would talk to you. He was liked by everyone in the Cabinet Office where he was called "son".

One of the Marines called him "Radar" because if you told him to pick you up from somewhere, he would be able to find you. Sturrup and I started to work on the FLAMINGO at the same time which was in March 1980. It was his request to be on that ship.

Anytime anyone wanted to laugh, he was the person to look for, his voice was unique.

You were liked Sturrup – God bless your soul, Rest in Peace.

David Tucker

Tucker was a Marine Seaman and Gunman on the Ship. He was a very hard-working young man. I can recall a trip when I was helping him load his 20mm gun, I got my finger badly mashed. He was very concerned.

On the same trip, we captured a boat laden and sinking with drugs. He slipped on his knife cutting his thigh badly and suffered from pain for days.

He was the type of person who liked seeing people happy. n His favorite song was, "Special Lady" by Ray Goodman and Brown.

God bless your soul Tucker, may you Rest in Peace.

Edward Williams

Williams was the quietest person I ever met. He had a meek and mild personality. I never heard him say harsh words at any time. The last thing I heard him say was "Farrington, why aren't we going to Ragged Island anymore?" He was so sad.

Anything you asked him to do, he did it. He feared the water but was a good Seaman.

May your soul Rest in Peace Williams.

All photos of the heros curtesy of rbdf.gov.bs/the-flamingo-incident

A Daring Night's Journey
Arrival at Ragged Island
Sunday, May 11th, 1980

A Daring Night's Journey
to Ragged Island

Guided only by the light on the Cay, we traveled on to Ragged Island. Commander Rolle ordered for all the lights on the boat to be turned off. The only light on the boat was provided by Miller who was smoking packs of Cuban cigarettes against the compass for light.

We had to travel down the shallow brooks to avoid being caught if followed. It was dangerous traveling without lights, but this was a chance we had to take. After a while, Miller ran out of cigarettes, so Kirby's computerized watch was used. It lasted for some time and when it went out as well, matches were then used.

It was so cold that night; a night one could never forget. Less than six hours prior, I was on board our ship with my fellow crewmen, now four of them and the ship were gone. We were filled with disbelief, fear, great sadness, and more than anything else, we were trying to stay alive because the lights in the distance were seeming to be getting closer. We were also very painful from being thrown about in the explosion, followed by the rapid swim to safety. Mentally we were not desiring food, but our bodies needed sustenance. We had not eaten the entire day and so we were very hungry.

Arrival at Ragged Island

It was a still and quiet night when we arrived at Ragged Island. When we got ashore, we all kissed the ground. It was a great relief to be on land again. I looked at my watch. It was 1:00 a.m.

Kirby and Wallace, who were originally from Duncan Town, told us about a track road that would take us into the settlement from where we were. With the darkness of the night as our cover, we set off on foot, still escorting our prisoners, to go to Duncan Town. All the residents were asleep and we spent the night at a police officer's resident. The police officer's name was Charles Rolle. Commander Rolle tried repeatedly to make contact with the Base at Coral Harbour in Nassau but communication was very poor on the island. It was not until the morning hours that he was able to send a telegram using Morse code, to inform our superiors about the tragic events and daring attacks by the Cubans.

Sunday, May 11th, 1980 – Mother's Day At Ragged Island

That morning was Sunday, May 11th, Mother's Day. It was the most painful bit of news for mothers to hear on Mother's Day!

Early that morning, Kirby's aunt came to him crying after hearing the news. The street soon became full of people who showed their concern. The resident nurse checked us over to determine our medical condition. Saunders had a bullet in his arm. I had terrible pain in my shoulder, and Clarke had his arm injured.

"The planes are coming," someone shouted and we were all ready to take cover. First came a big Cuban military transport plane. It landed with men at the airport but they did not come into the settlement. The worst of it all was when two MIG jets came zooming down on Duncan Town just as they had done on the HMBS Flamingo, only this time they did not fire. They did, however, terrorize the community that Sunday.

People were afraid to leave home to go to church to worship. Children, teenagers, and adults watched their cruelty as they imitated their attack. Hearing the jets again brought great fear to all of us because we knew and saw the damage they had done to the FLAMINGO.

Later that morning a helicopter just as the one that had flown over the FLAMINGO, seemed as if it was trying to scare everyone on the Island to death. Although some reports of the event state that the helicopter landed at one point on the island, the occupants of the helicopter never disembarked but remained on board with guns drawn as the aircraft hovered very low.

Commander Swinley and the Commissioner of Police had arrived on Ragged Island on a Bahamian DC3 aircraft to look into the situation and to the wellbeing of the surviving crew members. They were witnesses to the assault by the Cuban helicopter and aircraft on the community and they contacted Nassau to report what was going on. They had come on the DC 3 to take us and the prisoners back to Nassau but the Cuban jetfighters were delaying our departure.

The assault by the Cuban aircraft continued for some three hours. Around 2:30 p.m. that afternoon two air force jets believed to be American flew over the island. After their appearance, the Cuban jetfighters left the area and we were finally able to take off from Ragged Island.

American fighters saved Ragged Island residents

AN EYEWITNESS said Monday that five Cuban military aircraft buzzed Duncan Town on Ragged Island for four and a half hours Sunday and broke off only after two US military jets showed up.

The witness, Louis Pintard, said the Cuban aircraft two MiG jet fighters, two large transport planes and a helicopter made repeated mock strafing runs over Duncan Town, where survivors of a Bahamian patrol boat sunk by Cuban MiGs on Saturday and eight Cuban fishermen had been taken.

Mr Pintard, speaking in Nassau after being flown here in a news photographer's plane, said the Cuban aircraft concentrated on the police residence building, where the fishermen were being detained, and on the Cuban fishing boat in custody.

He said the 150 residents of Duncan Town were very alarmed over the Cuban buzzing and appealed to the Marines to release the Cuban prisoners.

The aircraft, he said, were flying so low "it seemed you could almost touch them."

He said that two chartered aircraft with top Bahamian police and defence officials had landed on the island, along with a chartered DC-3 aircraft which was to pick up the prisoners and the surviving patrol boat crew.

But the persistent mock strafing runs prevented the Bahamian planes from taking off, he said.

He said that the helicopter landed on a beach between two coconut groves at 10 am and remained on the ground for 10 minutes before taking off again, but no one got out.

Mr Pintard said that at precisely 2 pm two American jet fighters made an appearance and circled the town.

He said the Cuban military aircraft quickly left the area.

Mr Pintard said that police officials at Duncan Town identified the two fighters as American military warplanes, but which branch was not immediately known.

He said that a British destroyer (HMS Eskimo) also showed up off the eastern coast of Ragged Island at 7 pm. But by this time all had returned to normal.

The Cuban fishing boat was one of two that had been taken in tow by the Bahamian vessel after being captured for fishing in Bahamian waters.

After the patrol boat Flamingo was sunk, the survivors and all the Cuban fishermen were packed into one fishing boat. The other was abandoned at sea.

JLP alarmed

KINGSTON, JAMAICA (CANA) – Opposition Jamaica Labour Party (JLP) leader Edward Seaga, said today his party "views with alarm" the bombing of a Bahamian force vessel Saturday by a Cuban plane.

Speaking at a press conference, Seaga said subject to the facts of the case being proven, it appeared that the Bahamian forces were dealing with poachers in their own territorial waters.

In this case, he said, Cuba would have committed an act of aggression, and an act against the territorial integrity of another state, as well as an act against a fellow Thir...

Photo courtesy of the Department of Archives

Arrival in Nassau
Talk of the Nation and the World

Arrival in Nassau

I can recall the state that we arrived in Nassau very well. We were all dirty and bare feet. I had a baby diaper tied around my arm. My shoulder felt as if it had been dislocated.

There were policemen, Defence Force officers, reporters, and cameras all over the place. We were rushed off to the Coral Habour Base. Everyone was so sad, some of us even cried. I was one of those who cried.

It was terrible. We left on a ship with 19 men and came back on a plane with only 15. I was moved to tears over the brevity of life. I had just relieved Smith from his shift, and in a matter of minutes, he had been gone forever. All four of them were.

Some of the crew left for home while Dencil Clarke, Willard Saunders, myself, and a few others were taken to the Princess Margret Hospital for checkups. By this time, the hospital grounds were full of family, friends, the public, and the press, all wanting to see us, some genuinely concerned about our wellbeing, others just wanting to see. The press, in search of the story.

AIRPORT SCENE — The returning survivors of the ill-fated Defence Force vessel Flamingo sunk by Cuban fighters on Saturday returned to Nassau Sunday afternoon from Ragged Island in a charter Kwin-Air DC-3. Eight Cuban fishermen were also brought back for trial on poaching charges and were escorted to a waiting police van (left) while a mini-bus (centre) took the Defence Force men back to the Coral Harbour Defence Force Base. Security police and plainclothes men guard the area in foreground.

Photo courtesy of the Department of Archives

Talk of The Nation and The World

Every inhabited island in The Bahamas gave their regrets for the loss of lives and the HMBS Flamingo. There were also international radio and television broadcasts, and newspaper articles in which the world talked, wrote and expressed their views on the sinking of the FLAMINGO and the tragic deaths. Canada's Globe and Mail in particular, featured a lengthy article on Tuesday, May 13th under the caption, **"Inexcusable bombing."** The article spoke in detail about the incident, Cuba's apology and The Bahamas' response to it. A day earlier, The Tribune reported that Prime Minister Margaret Thatcher's government in Brittan had also condemned Cuba's actions.

Outside of the news coverage, letters of condolence came into the Royal Bahamas Defence Force from people of all ages and from every sector of society. They came also from neighbouring Caribbean countries, as well as other countries, namely our neighbor to the North; the United States of America, as well as Canada and the United Kingdom.

Immediately following our arrival back in Nassau, Commander Rolle was summoned to an urgent meeting on National Security where he reported to the Acting Prime Minister, Arthur Hanna, and other leading government officials on the entire proceedings. Prime Minister Pindling was out of the country attending a ceremony in London. On receiving the news, he canceled his trip and made arrangements to return home.

By this time, the Cuban government had made the statement that the incident had been a matter of mistaken identity. They said that they had taken the HMBS Flamingo for a pirate ship. Acting Prime Minister, Arthur

D. Hanna in speaking to reporters late Sunday night, May 11th, 1980, dismissed the 'Pirate Ship' claim.

The following day, Monday, May 12th, a delegation from the Cuban government arrived in Nassau for a meeting with our Bahamian government officials. The meeting lasted for three hours and the delegation returned to Cuba that same night. The Bahamas government's position on the attack was clearly stated to the Republic of Cuba by the Attorney General, Mr. Paul Adderley in a Note of Protest. The note specified The Bahamas' demand that the Government of the Republic of Cuba apologize to the Government and the people of the Commonwealth of The Bahamas for its violent acts of aggression. The note also demanded the assurance of the Cuban government that the sovereignty and the territorial integrity of The Bahamas would be respected and not violated in the future.

On Tuesday morning, the Cuban government informed The Bahamas government that their delegation would be retuning that afternoon to continue discussions. This message was followed by a telex message from the Cuban Foreign Affairs Minister, Isidoro Malmierca to the Government of The Bahamas advising that the delegation would in fact not be returning that afternoon to resume discussions as was scheduled. The message stated that the delegation needed more time to examine all of the information received and to prepare for the next round of discussions.

Meanwhile, Prime Minister Pindling, now back in The Bahamas, paid a visit to the Base at Coral Harbour. He met Royal Bahamas Defence Force officers and praised the crew of the HMBS Flamingo when it was attacked, for our display of bravery and devotion to duty. During his visit, he also held an on the spot press conference. The Bahamas government was outraged. The Prime Minister wanted a response, but he wanted also to maintain good relations with Cuba. He said the Government of The Bahamas was not going to be entering into a defence treaty with another country. He said in our experience, and in our region, it is better to not enter into a formal defence agreement and let the rightness of a cause determine the support you get.

But a lot was going on that Tuesday. That same day, the Bahamian government also learned of accusations being made by the Cuban government about The Bahamas being used by the CIA to orchestrate the arrest of the men on board the Cuban fishing vessels. Minister Paul

Adderley said in response to the accusation that the unprovoked attack on the HMBS Flamingo and the killing of Bahamians and the violation of Bahamian territory and the aerial harassment of the Duncan Town, Ragged Island community, had nothing to do with the Cuban-United States problem.

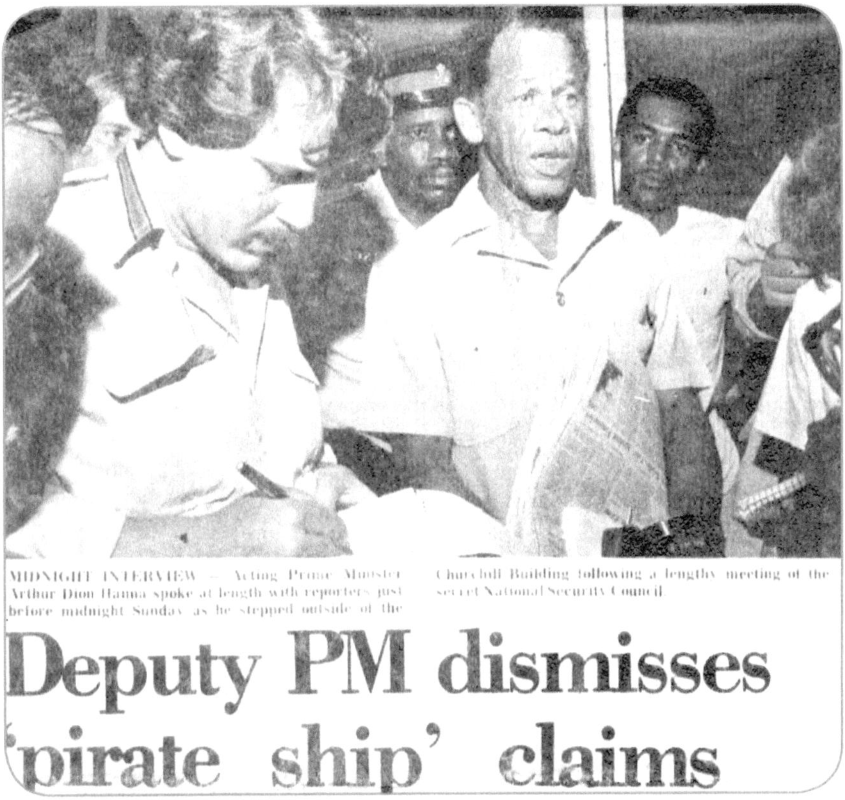

MIDNIGHT INTERVIEW — Acting Prime Minister Arthur Dion Hanna spoke at length with reporters just before midnight Sunday as he stepped outside of the Churchill Building following a lengthy meeting of the secret National Security Council.

Deputy PM dismisses 'pirate ship' claims

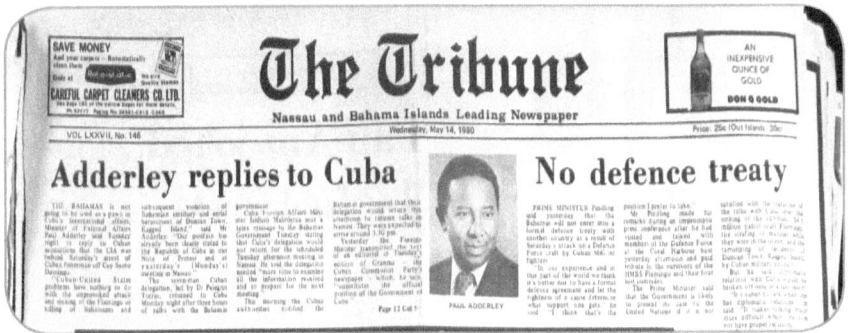

rbdf.gov.bs/the-flamingo-incident

SAVE MONEY

CAREFUL CARPET CLEANERS CO. LTD.

The Tribune

Nassau and Bahama Islands Leading Newspaper

VOL LXXVII, No. 146 | Wednesday, May 14, 1980 | Price: 25c (Out Islands 30c)

AN INEXPENSIVE OUNCE OF GOLD

DON Q GOLD

Adderley replies to Cuba

PAUL ADDERLEY

No defence treaty

Courtesy of the Department of Archives

PRIME MINISTER PINDLING met with members of the Defence Force yesterday and praised the men who were aboard the Flamingo when it was attacked Saturday for their "display of bravery and devotion to duty."

Mr Pindling particularly praised Captain Amos Rolle who was in command of Flamingo at the time of attack.

"The circumstances must have been most difficult, but, under fire Mr Rolle and his men never once lost their nerve, never once panicked, and despite the considerable provocation, never sought to resort to barbarism which is one way one can describe the acts that were perpetrated against them," the Prime Minister said.

Courtesy of the Department of Archives

The country was unified in its grief. Our fellow civil servants and other Bahamian workers, all wore black on Tuesday, May 13th, as a symbol of unity. The somberness lasted for some time. In another grand gesture, one of the major Unions in the country suspended its protests against the Government. Although it was not said, the intent was likely to allow the Government to give its full attention to the situation which was of such grave, national importance.

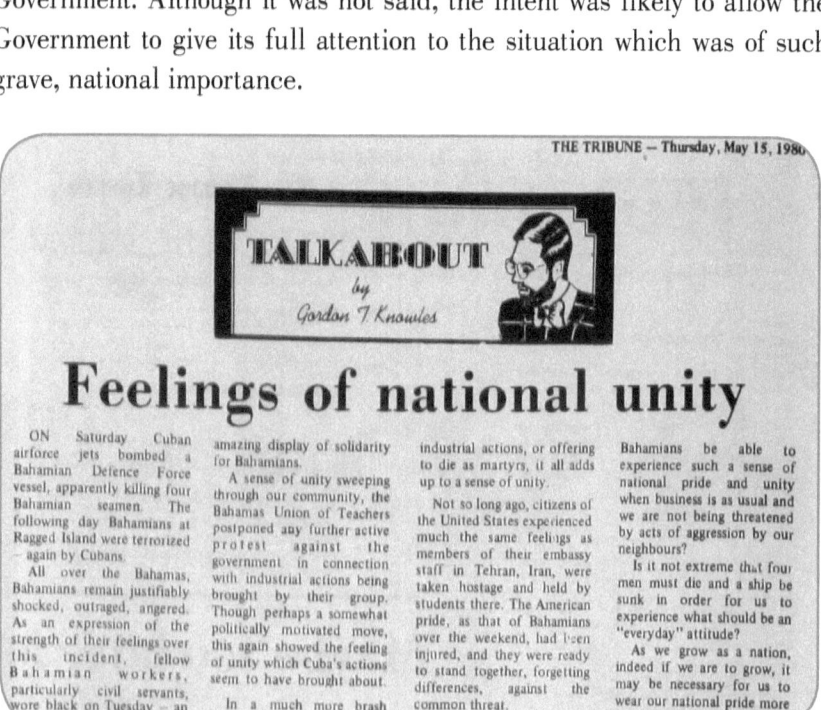

THE TRIBUNE — Thursday, May 15, 1980

TALKABOUT
by Gordon J Knowles

Feelings of national unity

ON Saturday Cuban airforce jets bombed a Bahamian Defence Force vessel, apparently killing four Bahamian seamen. The following day Bahamians at Ragged Island were terrorized again by Cubans.

All over the Bahamas, Bahamians remain justifiably shocked, outraged, angered. As an expression of the strength of their feelings over this incident, fellow Bahamian workers, particularly civil servants, wore black on Tuesday – an amazing display of solidarity for Bahamians.

A sense of unity sweeping through our community, the Bahamas Union of Teachers postponed any further active protest against the government in connection with industrial actions being brought by their group. Though perhaps a somewhat politically motivated move, this again showed the feeling of unity which Cuba's actions seem to have brought about.

In a much more brash statement, members of the industrial actions, or offering to die as martyrs, it all adds up to a sense of unity.

Not so long ago, citizens of the United States experienced much the same feelings as members of their embassy staff in Tehran, Iran, were taken hostage and held by students there. The American pride, as that of Bahamians, over the weekend, had been injured, and they were ready to stand together, forgetting differences, against the common threat.

Bahamians be able to experience such a sense of national pride and unity when business is as usual and we are not being threatened by acts of aggression by our neighbours?

Is it not extreme that four men must die and a ship be sunk in order for us to experience what should be an "everyday" attitude?

As we grow as a nation, indeed if we are to grow, it may be necessary for us to wear our national pride more boldly and allow the world to

Courtesy of the Department of Archives

The Batelco Union, the union for The Bahamas' telecommunications company was also prepared to instruct its members to cease handling all telegraphic and telephone traffic with Cuba until the current dispute was satisfactorily resolved.

Certainly, the tragedy was on everybody's mind and everybody's tongue. I was on Bay Street one day a week later, our business center in Nassau, and people looked at me differently. They asked me all types of questions, they wanted to know what happened. They wanted to hear the story again and again. Back home in Eleuthera, people visited and showed concern. Some people made jokes while others quoted from the Bible.

My mother and family were so glad to see me. I was very glad to see them also. During the catastrophe, I thought I would never see my family again.

Memorial Services
Reparation for our Sons and our Ship
Saying Thank You

Memorial Services

Memorial services were held all over The Bahamas for the four Marines. The first one I attended was at Our Lady's Church, Nassau. The service was held for Austin Smith who was a member there. A service was held for Fenrick Sturrup at Christ the King Church, Worker House, Nassau where he was a member. There was also a State Memorial Service at Clifford Park, Nassau. Other services were held at Christ Church Cathedral, Nassau and the Methodist Church, Alice Town, Eleuthera.

There were many more services held around the country but I cannot recall them all. The families were in mourning, and the nation mourned with them. It was a tragic loss of life. The life of four dedicated young men; Smith, Sturrup, Tucker, and Williams. A time to die…

Scenes from Clifford Park at the Memorial Service

The country officially mourned the deaths of the 4 fallen Defence Force marines during a ceremony at Clifford Park on Sunday 1 June 1980. In attendance were Senior Commander Amos Rolle, the Commanding Officer along with the fourteen (14) additional surviving crew members of HMBS FLAMINGO and the families of the fallen men.
(Photo by Mr. E. Bruce Delancey)

Photo by Al Rahming. Pictured: Oscar Miller, Gregory Curry, Cladwell Farrington, Anthony Russell, Eugene Thompson, John Wallace and Whitfield Neely

And throughout the years that followed, the memorials continued to be held and are still held on the anniversary of the incident; at sea (above and left) as well as on land. Successive governments have also paid tribute to the four men who lost their lives for their country.

Photo by Cladwell Farrington 2019

At the Royal Bahamas Defence Force Base at Coral Harbour, a memorial monument was erected in their honour. **rbdf.gov.bs/the-flamingo-incident"**

Other tributes that have been done include a recent project by Bahamian artist Kishan Munroe. Munroe researched and painted a series of paintings depicting the events of that ill-fated weekend incident. One of

the paintings in the series is entitled ***"The Sinking of HMBS Flamingo"**.*
The painting was done in 2014 in oil and acrylic on canvas.

"The Sinking of HMBS Flamingo," by Kishan Munroe.

Reparation for Our Sons
and Our Ship

Negotiations were going on between our government and the government of Cuba for months. The talks were very confusing and delicate. Cuba, after calling the attack a mistake, accused The Bahamas of working with the CIA to attack them.

During one of their trips to Nassau, Cuban Government Officials were met with a strong protest against them in the form of a demonstration at the Nassau International Airport.

Eventually, the Cuban Government accepted responsibility for the attack and paid compensation for the loss of the fallen marines, the ship, and her supplies. $100,000 was paid to each of the families of the four men and $5 million was paid for the HMBS Flamingo.

The question that came to my mind was, I wonder if they know how precious life is. Life cannot be valued in terms of money. However, we must learn to forgive.

The Tribune

Nassau and Bahama Islands Leading Newspaper

VOL. LXXVII, No. 147   Thursday, May 15, 1980   Price: 25c (Out Islands: 30c)

FOR THE BEST IN DRY CLEANING visit "Jiffy"
WE PICK UP AND DELIVER

NATURALLY BEAUTIFUL WOOD with CABOT'S CREOSOTE STAINS
Bahamian Paint Supply

Havana team pays $80,000 bond

INQUEST INTO DEATHS

Demonstrators jeer Cubans

ANGRY CROWD AT AIRPORT — Angry Bahamian demonstrators carry placards at the airport and completely surround the two limousines carrying the seventeen Cuban delegation to the Ministry of External Affairs building in Nassau. The Cubans faced verbal abuse, taunts and angry insults from the crowd, which numbered about 400. (Photo: DEREK SMITH)

Call for road safety

Bahamas rejects Cuban message

Courtesy of the Department of Archives

Saying Thank You

A great deal has been said in the days, weeks, months, and years that followed the Flamingo Incident about the four marines who died. But what about the fifteen men who survived? We have lived with the scars on our bodies, in our minds, and our hearts. Some of the men have received commendations over the years, but they needed so much more.

Among those receiving recognition were, first of all, Commander Amos Rolle. He was lauded for his bravery and exemplary behavior in leading the officers and crewmen to safety in the face of enemy fire. He received personal congratulations from Prime Minister Lynden Pindling on the afternoon of Tuesday, May 13th, 1980.

On August 29th, 1996, I received the Royal Bahamas Defence Force Traumatic Service Decoration. The presentation was also made by Prime Minister Pindling at Government House. (*Photo left*)

Whitfield Neely, now Captain Neely and the only of us remaining on the Force, this year received the Queen's New Year's honor.

Outside of these commendations, and the recognition given to different groupings of the men at the annual memorial ceremonies, very little has been given or done for the survivors of the HMBS Flamingo.

From the beginning, immediately following the incident, all of the energy and emotions were centered on the four crewmen who were lost, and rightly so. They deserved to be honored and remembered and their families ministered to, but the needs of the other fifteen men were sadly overlooked. Those of us who had wounds were patched up and sent home and expected to return to work as normal, as if the terrible incident of May 10th, 1980, had not happened to us as well. We did not receive a proper medical check-up. There was no Psychiatric evaluation done to see how the event may have affected us, nor were we afforded any kind of counseling; grief, or otherwise. There was also no compensation given to us with which we may have been able to pay for these things for ourselves. The only financial remuneration we received was the estimated value of the possessions we had with us. I received seventy-five dollars.

When we returned to Active duty, we did not have a ship to work on. We were instead given assignments on the base. Two weeks after the sinking of the HMBS Flamingo, Dencil Clarke, Maynard Miller, and I were asked to accompany the crew of the Acklins to take it around Nassau Harbour to the shipyard for repairs. The boat was a 50-foot craft, one of the four original crafts used by the marine police until the amalgamation into the Royal Bahamas Defense Force.

We had no choice but to obey. On the sea, everything was going fine. We were all below when a cry rang out. Fire!

As I heard, I said, "My Lord, not again!" We made every effort to put out the fire but with no success.

"Abandon Ship!" Captain Rodger Rolle ordered and we jumped overboard. We were in the area of South Ocean Beach Hotel, an area known to be heavily populated by sharks. The boat's engine was still running and it was going around and around as if it would run us over. A boat with some fishermen appeared out of nowhere and rescued us. By this time, the 'San Salvador' was engulfed in thick, black smoke. I was choking from the smoke, tired and upset but thankful that we all made it that time.

The events of May 10th, 1980 were life-changing for us. Some of the survivors struggled to get their lives back to normal. Some were successful while for others, it continued to be a challenge. Sadly, Miller was one of those who was not able to do so. He became depressed and remained in that state until his passing. He was buried in his hometown of Hatchet Bay, Eleuthera without any representation from the Force or recognition of his time of service, except for a memorial service held in Nassau which was attended by a few Royal Bahamas Defense Force personnel.

Over the years, I have sought some form of legislation for benefits from the government to be put in place for the remaining survivors who needed assistance. I wrote letters to successive governments pleading for consideration to be given to the situation but I did not receive a reply. I also wrote a letter to The Editor addressing our plight and the manner the survivors seem to be forgotten.

Today, the number of remaining survivors is decreasing, as some have since passed on but I am still hoping that the cry would be heard. In addition to Chief Petty Officer Oscar Maynard Miller, others who have died include Acting Sub Lieutenant Wilfred Sands, Chief Petty Officer Leo Kirby, and Senior Commander Amos Rolle, commanding officer of HMBS Flamingo at the time of the incident.

www.ingramcontent.com/pod-product-compliance
Lightning Source LLC
Chambersburg PA
CBHW021508210526
45463CB00002B/950